Who Was
Queen Victoria?

Who Was Queen Victoria?

by Jim Gigliotti

illustrated by Max Hergenrother

Penguin Workshop

For my sister, another Victoria with an indomitable spirit—JG

For my queen, Jeanean. May the monarchy reside in our home for all time—MH

PENGUIN WORKSHOP
An Imprint of Penguin Random House LLC, New York

Text copyright © 2014, 2022 by Jim Gigliotti.
Illustrations copyright © 2014 by Max Hergenrother.
Cover illustration copyright © 2014 by Penguin Random House LLC. All rights reserved.
Published by Penguin Workshop, an imprint of Penguin Random House LLC, New York.
PENGUIN and PENGUIN WORKSHOP are trademarks of Penguin Books Ltd.
WHO HQ & Design is a registered trademark of Penguin Random House LLC.
Printed in the USA.

Visit us online at www.penguinrandomhouse.com.

Library of Congress Control Number: 2014944569

ISBN 9780448481821   20 19 18 17 16 15 14 13 12

Contents

Who Was
Queen Victoria?

Nothing was out of the ordinary when eighteen-year-old Princess Victoria went to bed on the evening of Monday, June 19, 1837. She fell asleep in Kensington Palace in London, in the room she shared with her mother, the Duchess of Kent. She had always shared a room with her mother. Her mother never allowed her to be alone.

At six o'clock the next morning, though, Victoria's world changed. She woke up to hear her mother say that two men had arrived at the palace. They wished to see Victoria.

The men were the archbishop of Canterbury and the lord chamberlain. The archbishop of Canterbury was the leader of the Church of England. The lord chamberlain was the top

official in the royal household, where the king lived.

Victoria put on her dressing gown and went to her sitting room. The men came in, and the lord chamberlain knelt before her. Victoria knew what that meant: Her uncle, King William IV, had died.

Victoria extended her hand, and the lord chamberlain kissed it. "The king died at twelve minutes past two o'clock in the morning," the lord chamberlain said. Princess Victoria was now Queen Victoria. She was the queen of the United Kingdom.

"Since it has pleased Providence to place me in this station," Victoria wrote in her journal later that night, "I shall do my utmost to fulfill my duty towards my country."

Although Victoria was only eighteen, she had been preparing for her role since she was eleven years old. That was when she became the next in line to the throne.

"I am very young and perhaps in many, though not in all things, inexperienced," the queen wrote, "but I am sure that very few have more real goodwill and more real desire to do what is fit and right than I have."

Victoria did what she felt was fit and right for more than sixty-three years as queen. She had the second-longest reign of any king or queen in Britain's history. She helped maintain peace and prosperity in her country, and she ruled at a time when exciting new discoveries were made in many fields. Victoria was so important to this time period that it has been named after her: the Victorian era.

Before any of that, however, one of Victoria's first declarations as queen was that her bed be moved into her own room. She would not share a room with her mother any longer.

The king was dead. Long live the queen.

Chapter 1
Childhood

When Princess Victoria was seven years old, she went for long carriage rides in the countryside outside London, England, with her grandmother, who was visiting from Saxe-Coburg-Saalfeld in what is now Germany. Victoria loved her grandmother and enjoyed the beautiful horses, but she didn't care to be driven around the countryside. Like many young girls, she later admitted in her journal, she "preferred running about."

Victoria loved running and playing with her dog, a King Charles spaniel named Dash.

Other times, she played with her doll collection. She loved dolls so much that she had more than one hundred of them! Victoria had a full schedule of schoolwork, too, and enjoyed some of her academic subjects more than others. She was fascinated by history, and excellent at learning languages.

That all may sound as if Victoria had a typical childhood. She didn't. Certainly anyone born into royalty will have a different upbringing. Victoria, however, had a particularly uncommon childhood, and it was not an especially happy one.

Victoria was born as Alexandrina Victoria in Kensington Palace in London on May 24, 1819.

Her father was Prince Edward, the Duke of Kent.
Her mother was Victoire, the Duchess of Kent.
Sometimes the newborn's family called her "Drina"
at home, but mostly she was just "Victoria."

Victoria was only eight months old when her father died unexpectedly. The duke caught a severe cold, which turned to pneumonia. He died on January 23, 1820.

Victoria grew up without a father. Her mother, the Duchess of Kent, did not remarry, but she did ask a close friend of her husband's, Sir John Conroy, to help run the household. He became a financial adviser and secretary to the duchess. Victoria did not trust Conroy—and with good reason.

SIR JOHN CONROY

After her father's death, Victoria's mother made a plan with Conroy. They both hoped to keep young Victoria so dependent on them that their opinions would come to matter more than her own. Conroy wanted power. He could never be king because he was not born into the right family, but he was determined to exert great influence on Victoria.

The atmosphere in the palace was one of

drama and intrigue in the early years of Victoria's life. If Victoria's uncle, King William IV, died before she turned eighteen, her mother would become queen regent and rule the United Kingdom on Victoria's behalf. If he died after she turned eighteen, Victoria would be queen. Either way, Conroy and the duchess wanted to be in control.

Victoria was not allowed to make or play with friends her age. She was never left alone, not even at night. That's why she shared a bedroom with her mother. She did not talk to adults unless either Conroy, her mother, or her governess also was present. She couldn't even walk up and down the stairs in the palace by herself! She was required to hold her governess's hand on the staircase right up until the time she became queen.

Victoria did not have many childhood friends, and she was the only child the Duke and Duchess of Kent had together. Victoria had a half sister, Feodore, but Feodore was eleven years older. Instead, Victoria was closest to her governess, Miss Louise

GOVERNESS MISS LOUISE LEHZEN

Lehzen. A governess is a woman who helps raise the children in a private home. When Victoria was five years old, Miss Lehzen became her governess. By then, Victoria had shown that she could sometimes be stubborn, impatient, and rude. Later in life, Victoria diplomatically called it being "passionate."

Miss Lehzen quickly taught Victoria to be polite and to apologize when she was too "passionate." But Miss Lehzen also quietly encouraged Victoria to maintain her independence from Conroy and her mother.

Although Conroy and the Duchess of Kent wanted Victoria to be dependent on them, Victoria developed an incredibly strong will and rebelled by becoming fiercely independent. That

would serve her well in her adult life as queen.

Victoria's childhood wasn't all bad, of course. She was very close to Miss Lehzen, and she was often pampered. For her fourteenth birthday, the king gave a ball in her honor. Victoria danced all night and didn't get home until half past midnight. "I was very much amused," she wrote before going to sleep.

NEXT IN LINE

AT THE TIME OF VICTORIA'S BIRTH IN 1819, HER GRANDFATHER, GEORGE III, WAS KING OF THE UNITED KINGDOM. IT WAS CALLED THE UNITED KINGDOM BECAUSE IN 1707, ENGLAND (WHICH ALREADY INCLUDED THE SMALL COUNTRY OF WALES) AND SCOTLAND JOINED TO CREATE GREAT BRITAIN. IN 1801, GREAT BRITAIN ADDED

KING GEORGE III

IRELAND TO "UNITE THE KINGDOM." (MOST OF
IRELAND REGAINED INDEPENDENCE IN 1922;
NORTHERN IRELAND REMAINS PART OF THE UNITED
KINGDOM.)

VICTORIA WAS FIFTH IN THE LINE OF
SUCCESSION AFTER THREE UNCLES (THE PRINCE
OF WALES, THE DUKE OF YORK, AND THE DUKE OF
CLARENCE) AND HER FATHER, THE DUKE OF KENT.

THE PRINCE OF WALES OFFICIALLY BECAME
KING GEORGE IV WHEN GEORGE III DIED IN 1820,
ONLY SIX DAYS AFTER VICTORIA'S OWN FATHER
DIED.

THE DUKE OF YORK, WHOSE NAME WAS
FREDERICK, DIED IN 1827. GEORGE IV DIED
SHORTLY THEREAFTER IN 1830, AND THE DUKE OF
CLARENCE REIGNED AS WILLIAM IV FOR SEVEN
YEARS BEFORE VICTORIA WAS CROWNED QUEEN.

Chapter 2
Becoming Queen

Victoria was eleven years old when King George IV died in 1830, leaving her next in line for the throne. She didn't know that, though, until Miss Lehzen went over the family tree with her one day. "I'm nearer to the throne than I thought," Victoria said.

KING GEORGE IV

Victoria liked her uncle George IV, but saw that he was unnecessarily extravagant and was unpopular with his subjects. Many of them did not mourn his death. She liked her uncle William IV, too, but he would soon prove to be an ineffective king. The monarchy had become unpopular in England because of George IV and William IV, and Victoria vowed she would change that. "I will be good," she famously proclaimed to Miss Lehzen.

KING WILLIAM IV

Aware of her future responsibilities, Victoria took her education seriously. Her family originally was from Germany, but she learned to speak perfect English in addition to German. She also spoke French and Italian, and was well schooled in history and the arts.

Victoria's favorite uncle, Leopold, offered advice on politics and helped her prepare to become queen. Leopold was like a second father to Victoria. "He is indeed like my real father, as I have none!" she wrote in her journal. "He alone can give me good advice on every thing."

Victoria and Leopold began corresponding by letter in 1828. Even after Leopold became the first king of Belgium in 1831, uncle and niece

LEOPOLD, KING OF BELGIUM

frequently wrote letters to each other until the king's death in 1865.

In 1832, when Victoria was thirteen years old, she began keeping a journal. She wrote almost every night until shortly before her death in 1901.

From her journals, we know young Victoria began taking note of the people and the places over which she would reign one day. She wrote about a trip to Wales in 1832, and about miners, and about children living in poverty. She hoped that one day, as queen, she would be able to help and to serve her subjects well.

The trips to Wales and other places in Britain were Conroy's idea. He and the Duchess of Kent thought it would be a good experience for Victoria to travel. They didn't want to keep her from becoming queen, they just wanted to be the ones to have the most influence over her.

ORKNEY ISLANDS

SCOTLAND

IRELAND

ENGLAND

WALES

Victoria, though, would not hand over any of her authority to Conroy or her mother. One day, when Victoria was seventeen, Conroy tried to get a written promise from her that she would one day make him her private secretary. Victoria refused. She would not be bullied.

In August 1836, King William IV turned seventy-one years old. He was dying, and he knew it. William IV loved his niece and had tried to expose her to life as a monarch so she would be ready to become queen. But Conroy and the

duchess made excuses much of the time to keep her away from her uncle, King William IV.

That infuriated the king. At his seventy-first birthday party, he embarrassed the duchess and vowed to hang on to the crown at least until Victoria turned eighteen. "I trust in God that my life may be spared for nine months longer," he said in a speech before all the guests at the large banquet. "I should then have the satisfaction of leaving the exercise of the royal authority to the personal authority of that young lady, heiress

presumptive to the crown, and not in the hands of a person now near me, who is surrounded by evil advisers and is herself incompetent to act with propriety in the situation in which she would be placed."

William IV succeeded. One month after the princess turned eighteen in May 1837, William IV died, and Victoria began her reign.

Chapter 3
Controversy

Only hours after becoming queen, Victoria awed political leaders in Britain with her poise while delivering a statement formally accepting the throne before the Privy Council. The Privy Council was a group of senior politicians that acted as special advisors to the queen. "She not merely filled her chair," the Duke of Wellington later said, "she filled the room."

Clearly, Victoria was up to the challenge of being the queen. Though she was only eighteen years old, no more than five feet tall, and a woman working largely in a man's world, Victoria soon impressed members of Parliament with her grasp of the issues and a willingness to work hard.

Still, Victoria had a lot to learn. The new

queen relied heavily on the counsel of Lord Melbourne, who was the British prime minister at the time. The experienced Melbourne was fifty-eight years old when Victoria became queen. He had first been elected to Parliament in 1806.

LORD MELBOURNE

PARLIAMENT AND THE PM

PARLIAMENT IS THE GROUP OF POLITICIANS THAT MAKES AND PASSES LAWS IN GREAT BRITAIN. PARLIAMENT IS MADE UP OF THE HOUSE OF LORDS AND THE HOUSE OF COMMONS. THE MEMBERS OF THE HOUSE OF LORDS ARE APPOINTED, INCLUDING SOME BY THE MONARCH. THE MEMBERS OF THE HOUSE OF COMMONS ARE ELECTED BY THE CITIZENS OF THE UNITED KINGDOM.

THE PRIME MINISTER (PM) IS A MEMBER OF

THE HOUSE OF COMMONS AND IS THE MOST IMPORTANT POLITICIAN IN GREAT BRITAIN. TRADITIONALLY, HE OR SHE IS THE LEADER OF THE PARTY IN POWER. WHEN VICTORIA BECAME QUEEN, THE MAIN POLITICAL PARTIES IN GREAT BRITAIN WERE THE TORY PARTY AND THE WHIG PARTY. THE TORIES WERE CONSERVATIVE, OR LESS INTERESTED IN CHANGE THAN THE WHIGS. THE WHIGS WERE THE LIBERAL PARTY, INTERESTED IN MAKING CHANGES WITHIN THE GOVERNMENT. THE PRIME MINISTER APPOINTS CABINET MINISTERS, HELPS CREATE GOVERNMENT POLICY, AND MEETS REGULARLY WITH THE KING OR QUEEN TO GIVE AND RECEIVE ADVICE.

While Victoria welcomed Melbourne's advice, she did not rely on Conroy and her mother at all. Victoria moved Conroy and the duchess to the far end of the new, and expansive, Buckingham Palace and did not allow them any input into her affairs.

The duchess was not happy. Victoria told her mother she shouldn't be surprised "after the unaccountable manner in which [Conroy] behaved towards me, a short while before I came to the throne." The duchess complained about her rooms, too, and about her allowance. She and Victoria grew further apart.

Otherwise, though, Victoria was enjoying the perks of being the queen. She was young and single and outgoing. She enjoyed the parties, the dancing, and staying up late.

Victoria's official coronation came at Westminster Abbey one year later, on June 28, 1838. She woke up at four o'clock that morning.

The preparations for the event were noisy! By seven o'clock, she gave up hope for any more sleep. By ten o'clock, the procession from Buckingham Palace to the abbey had begun. More than four hundred thousand people lined the streets, cheering her on.

After Kings George IV and William IV, the British people were ready to embrace a young and energetic monarch, and Victoria was a popular queen at first. She squandered some of that goodwill rather quickly, however, in the Bedchamber Crisis of 1839.

That year, the Whig party lost power in

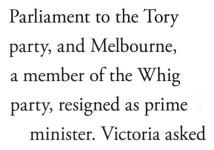

SIR ROBERT PEEL

Parliament to the Tory party, and Melbourne, a member of the Whig party, resigned as prime minister. Victoria asked Sir Robert Peel, a Tory, to form the new Parliament. As part of the deal, Peel insisted that Victoria replace her ladies of the bedchamber. Such assistants usually were the wives of noblemen, and would have been

Whigs from the previous regime. Peel felt that at least some of them should be members of the Tory party to reflect the new Parliament. Victoria refused.

She was being stubborn, but she also believed she was being bullied, just like Conroy had tried to bully her. She felt that it "was an attempt to see whether she could be led and managed like a child," she wrote to Melbourne.

Eventually, Peel declined to serve as prime minister, and Melbourne returned. As a result, the public thought that Victoria was "playing politics," while the role of a British monarch is officially to remain neutral. The queen's actions were criticized and, for a time, her popularity lessened.

LADIES OF THE BEDCHAMBER

A BEDCHAMBER IS A BEDROOM, BUT THE LADIES OF THE BEDCHAMBER DO NOT WORK IN THE QUEEN'S BEDROOM! THEY ARE ASSISTANTS WHO HELP THE QUEEN DURING PUBLIC CEREMONIES OR ON SPECIAL OCCASIONS. THEY ARE SOMETIMES THE QUEEN'S RELATIVES AND FRIENDS, WHO ARE ALSO HER COMPANIONS. LADIES OF THE BEDCHAMBER HELP WITH SHOPPING, LETTER WRITING, AND OTHER TASKS THE QUEEN ASSIGNS THEM.

THE WOMEN OF THE BEDCHAMBER ARE SIMILAR TO THE LADIES OF THE BEDCHAMBER, BUT THEY OFTEN LIVE AT THE PALACE, RATHER THAN COMING AND GOING FOR SPECIFIC SOCIAL EVENTS.

Chapter 4
Love Story

In 1836, Victoria's cousins Albert and Ernest visited from the German territory of Saxe-Coburg and Gotha. Albert and Ernest were the sons of the

ERNEST AND ALBERT

duke of Saxe-Coburg and Gotha. The duke was the older brother of Victoria's uncle Leopold.

In those days, royal marriages were often arranged and agreed upon by the extended family. Uncle Leopold thought one of his nephews would make a suitable husband for Victoria.

Victoria liked Prince Albert from the start. Shortly before Albert returned home, Victoria wrote to King Leopold. "I must thank you, my beloved Uncle, for the prospect of great happiness you have contributed to give me, in the person of dear Albert," she said.

Victoria praised Albert's kindness, sensibility, and friendliness. She thought he was rather handsome, too! "He has, besides, the most pleasing and delightful exterior and appearance you can possibly see," she said.

Albert was just three months younger than Victoria. He spoke German and English. He had a mustache and whiskers.

In some ways, Albert was just the opposite
of Victoria. He was nearly six feet tall, and he
towered over her. He liked to get to bed early
and wake up early, and she liked to stay up late
and sleep in. He was reserved, and Victoria was

outgoing. He was practical, and Victoria was stubborn. Still, sometimes opposites attract!

After Albert returned home, he and Victoria wrote many letters to each other, although Victoria made it clear to King Leopold that she had not agreed to any engagement. She might not even marry for several years, she told him. Victoria had an independent spirit and wanted to marry in her own due time.

But in October 1839, when Albert returned to England, it was clear he and Victoria were in love. "My heart is quite going," Victoria wrote in her journal.

By that time, Victoria was queen, and that posed a problem. Because Victoria was queen, any man would be considered to be "beneath her" (not worthy to marry her) so, according to the rules and manners of the time, no man could ask her to marry him.

Only five days into Albert's visit, Victoria sent for him. "You must be aware why I wished you to come here," she told him. "It would make me too happy if you would consent to what I wish." It wasn't exactly a traditional proposal, but Albert said yes. "I feel the happiest of human beings," Victoria wrote in her journal that night.

Victoria and Albert were married on February 10, 1840, at St. James's Palace in London. The fairy-tale wedding captivated the public. "I never saw such crowds of people as there were in the Park, and they cheered most enthusiastically," Victoria wrote about her carriage ride from Buckingham Palace to St. James's.

A twenty-one-gun salute marked the start of the carriage ride. The bride wore white lace, and

the twelve young girls who were her trainbearers wore white, too. Trumpets hailed the wedding procession, which included members of the royal family, Lord Melbourne, bridesmaids, the ladies of the bedchamber, the women of the bedchamber,

maids of honor, and more. When Victoria entered the chapel, the trumpets gave way to organ music.

Victoria and Albert promised to be true to each other until death . . . and they were.

THE QUEEN'S WEDDING DRESS

QUEEN VICTORIA WAS NOT THE FIRST BRIDE
TO WEAR A WHITE DRESS AT HER WEDDING, AND
SHE WASN'T EVEN THE FIRST MEMBER OF THE
ROYAL FAMILY TO DO SO. BUT SHE CERTAINLY DID
POPULARIZE THE WHITE WEDDING DRESS.

MOST BRIDES AT THE TIME WORE COLORED WEDDING DRESSES. WHITE FABRIC WAS TOO EXPENSIVE TO MAKE AND MAINTAIN. IT WAS A SYMBOL OF WEALTH AND STATUS TO OWN A DRESS THAT WAS DIFFICULT TO CLEAN AND THAT MIGHT ONLY BE WORN ONCE IN A LIFETIME. QUEEN VICTORIA CHOSE WHITE BECAUSE SHE WANTED TO INCORPORATE A PIECE OF LACE THAT WAS VERY SPECIAL TO HER INTO THE DRESS.

THE WEDDING OF VICTORIA AND ALBERT IN 1840 GOT SO MUCH ATTENTION THAT MANY OTHER BRIDES SOON FOLLOWED THE QUEEN'S EXAMPLE OF WEARING A WHITE DRESS ON THEIR WEDDING DAY. BY THE 1860S, WHITE BECAME THE FAVORED COLOR FOR WEDDING DRESSES, AND IT HAS BEEN EVER SINCE.

Chapter 5
Children and Family Life

It didn't take long after her wedding for Victoria to extend the line of succession to the throne. On November 21, 1840, she gave birth to Princess Victoria. The child would be called Vicky in the royal household.

One year later, on November 9, Albert Edward was born. He would be called Bertie. Seven more children followed—Alice, Alfred (called Alfie), Helena (called Lenchen), Arthur, Louise, Leopold, and Beatrice—giving Victoria and Albert a large family of five girls and four boys.

Victoria's family was the first royal family to live in Buckingham Palace. Although Victoria delighted in "court ceremonies, etiquette, and trivial formalities," as Albert once wrote to a

47

friend, she also loved to get away from royal duties and live as normal a family life as possible. She also preferred the countryside to London. So Victoria and Albert purchased and then rebuilt Osborne House on the Isle of Wight and Balmoral Castle in Scotland.

At Osborne House, Victoria and Albert built a separate cottage to help their children learn household skills—not that they ever needed them!

OSBORNE HOUSE

Education for their children was important
to Victoria and Albert. That included daughters
as well as sons. Unlike many ruling families that
educated only their sons, Victoria wanted her
daughters educated, just as she had been.

BUCKINGHAM PALACE

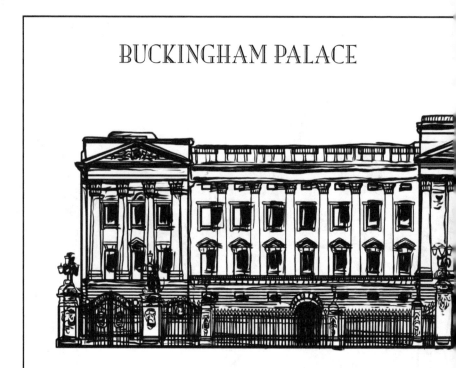

QUEEN VICTORIA WAS THE FIRST MONARCH TO LIVE IN BUCKINGHAM PALACE, WHICH IS STILL THE OFFICIAL LONDON RESIDENCE AND WORKPLACE OF THE REIGNING MONARCH.

THE PALACE ORIGINALLY WAS BUILT AS A HOME FOR THE DUKE OF BUCKINGHAM IN THE EARLY 1700S. KING GEORGE IV BEGAN TRANSFORMING IT INTO A ROYAL PALACE IN 1826, BUT BOTH HE AND KING WILLIAM IV DIED BEFORE IT WAS

COMPLETED. THE PALACE WAS ALMOST READY WHEN VICTORIA BECAME QUEEN IN 1837. ONE MONTH LATER, SHE MOVED IN.

BUCKINGHAM PALACE HAS 775 ROOMS, 92 OFFICES, AND 78 BATHROOMS. THE PALACE GARDEN IS THE LARGEST PRIVATE GARDEN IN LONDON. THE PALACE IS SO BIG, IT HAS ITS OWN POST OFFICE AND POLICE STATION!

Victoria's domestic life gradually came to include the Duchess of Kent as well. In 1842, Sir John Conroy, who had been given a title and a pension in return for staying away from court, retired. Miss Lehzen retired that same year after disagreeing with Albert over the raising of the children and her place in the household. Albert then helped Victoria to reconcile with her mother, and the queen and the duchess became close once again.

Later that same year, Victoria and Albert took a twenty-five-minute train ride out of London. Steam locomotives had been around since before Victoria's reign, but no British royal had ever traveled by train before.

Victoria wanted to see what it was like. She was "quite charmed" by the new way to travel, according to a letter she wrote to King Leopold.

She soon had her own royal train cars,
complete with modern luxuries. Hers was the first
in the world to have an on-board bathroom!

Chapter 6
Mourning

Victoria's large family meant that for a period of seventeen years, she spent much of the time pregnant and caring for infants. Albert was a doting father who enjoyed his children. But he also became more involved in the monarchy as time went on.

PRINCE ALBERT

At first, Albert was given only small duties such as helping Victoria blot her signature on official papers. Part of the reason was because the queen liked to do things her way. And part of it was because Albert came from Germany and

THE CHRISTMAS TREE

PRINCE ALBERT OFTEN IS CREDITED WITH "INVENTING" THE CHRISTMAS TREE. BUT THE TRADITION OF BRINGING AN EVERGREEN TREE OR WREATH INDOORS IN THE MIDDLE OF WINTER DEVELOPED IN GERMANY. THESE EARLY TREES SYMBOLIZED LIFE—BY STAYING GREEN DURING THE COLDEST MONTHS—AND WERE DECORATED WITH APPLES, NUTS, AND CANDIES AS GIFTS FOR THE CHILDREN OF THE HOUSE. WHEN PRINCE ALBERT INTRODUCED THIS GERMAN TRADITION TO VICTORIA AND THEIR CHILDREN IN THE EARLY 1840S, THE CUSTOM QUICKLY SPREAD TO OTHER WEALTHY FAMILIES WHO WERE EAGER TO FOLLOW THE TRENDS OF THE ROYAL FAMILY. THE CUSTOM EVENTUALLY SPREAD TO THE MIDDLE CLASSES AND WELL BEYOND THE UNITED KINGDOM.

spoke English with a German accent. The English people weren't quite ready to embrace their queen's foreign husband. Albert, in fact, did not have an official role or an official title. He was still Prince Albert.

Albert gradually took on more visible roles. He began attending meetings with Victoria's ministers and making public appearances.

In 1841, Melbourne resigned again. This time, Peel *did* take over as prime minister, and Albert succeeded Melbourne as the queen's most trusted political adviser.

Albert threw himself into his work, championing many causes, including an end to slavery around the world. He also was aware of how life was becoming more and more difficult for poor people in England. The Industrial Revolution—the growth of industry involving new machines, technologies, and factory work—had led to bigger and more crowded cities than society could keep up with. Steam engines, for example, meant that new machines could make material such as cloth faster than ever—faster than people working at home could—in factories and mills. Those factories needed workers, so

ALBERT'S MODEL LODGING HOUSE

more and more people from the countryside moved to work in the cities, which created poverty and overcrowding. Albert helped design experimental housing in order to provide better living conditions for the working poor.

Albert was fascinated by technological advances brought on by the Industrial Revolution. At Peel's

urging, he organized the Great Exhibition of 1851—a showcase for industry and technology. It featured thirteen thousand exhibits from around the world. Some exhibits featured new and useful machines, such as one that printed and folded envelopes. Other exhibits featured items of curiosity, such as the world-famous Koh-i-noor diamond, which eventually became part of the British crown jewels. There were sculptures from France and watches from Switzerland. There were even some velocipedes, which later became known as bicycles.

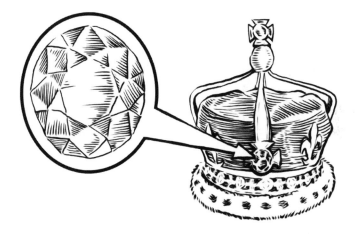

The exhibition was held in the Crystal Palace in London. It was a huge undertaking, but Albert worked hard to create an international showcase. It was overwhelmingly successful. The Great Exhibition was open for six months, and attracted more than six million visitors. Queen Victoria herself reportedly attended thirty-three times!

Up until this time, Albert performed his duties in an unofficial capacity. Then, in 1857, Victoria gave him the official title of prince consort.

Eventually, Albert's heavy workload began to take its toll, and his health declined. In 1860, Victoria's mother, too, was in poor health. The Duchess of Kent had surgery and became very weak as a result. She never fully recovered. When

Victoria's mother died in early 1861, the queen was devastated and went into a long period of grief. Albert, though in poor health himself, took on even more official duties. He became tired and weak and even more sick. On December 14, 1861, Queen Victoria's beloved husband, Albert, also died. He was just forty-two years old.

"My life as a happy one is ended," Victoria lamented to King Leopold.

Officially, the cause of Albert's death was typhoid fever, although the long period of illness leading up to his death indicates that it likely was something else, such as stomach cancer or Crohn's disease, which is an inflammation of the digestive tract.

For the rest of her life, Victoria mourned for Albert. She left his room exactly as it was. She had her servants put out clean clothes and towels for him every morning. It was as if she hoped her husband would soon return. She wore only black

dresses, clothes, and jewelry as an outward sign that she was still very sad without Albert.

CHARLES DICKENS

PRINCE ALBERT TRIED TO IMPROVE WORKING CONDITIONS IN ENGLAND, BUT IT WAS AUTHOR CHARLES DICKENS (1812–1870) WHO WAS PERHAPS THE LOUDEST VOICE FOR THE POOR IN THE VICTORIAN ERA. DICKENS WROTE STORIES THAT EXPOSED MANY OF ENGLAND'S SOCIAL PROBLEMS, SUCH AS POVERTY AND CHILD LABOR. (AS A CHILD, DICKENS HAD TO PASTE LABELS ON JARS OF SHOE POLISH IN A SHOE-BLACKING FACTORY.) HIS EARLY POVERTY DROVE HIM TO SUCCEED. HE WENT ON TO WRITE HUNDREDS OF SHORT STORIES

AND FIFTEEN NOVELS, INCLUDING *OLIVER TWIST*, *GREAT EXPECTATIONS*, *A TALE OF TWO CITIES*, AND *A CHRISTMAS CAROL*.

QUEEN VICTORIA WAS A FAN OF DICKENS. THEY MET IN PERSON ONCE, SHORTLY BEFORE DICKENS'S DEATH IN 1870. THE QUEEN GAVE HIM A BOOK SHE WROTE CALLED *LIFE IN THE SCOTTISH HIGHLANDS*. "HE TALKED OF HIS LATEST WORKS, OF AMERICA, THE STRANGENESS OF THE PEOPLE THERE, OF THE DIVISION OF CLASSES IN ENGLAND, WHICH HE HOPED WOULD GET BETTER IN TIME," THE QUEEN WROTE IN HER JOURNAL.

CHARLES DICKENS WAS THE GREATEST NOVELIST OF THE VICTORIAN ERA.

Chapter 7
Empress of India

For fifteen years after Albert's death, Victoria withdrew from public life. She appeared in public only to dedicate memorials to Albert or to unveil statues of him.

The public shared her grief and felt for Victoria. But her sadness seemed to grow over time and she became a woman lost in self-pity. By her own

admission, she didn't even like to see other people happy.

"I am ashamed of myself," she told one visitor in 1863. "I do feel less happy than I ought when I see people happy—so odd and wrong! I can't bear to look at a man and his wife walking together."

Clearly, her work was affected. She refused to give up her crown (to stop being queen), or to delegate her responsibilities to others. Sometimes, she wouldn't even meet with her prime ministers or with members of Parliament. She would communicate with them through servants, or she would eavesdrop on meetings from an adjoining room with the door open.

Victoria's withdrawal from public life at Buckingham Palace made some people angry. Others wondered why the United Kingdom even needed its queen, because England's economy was doing great without her. During this time, laws were passed that began to lessen the queen's direct political power.

Some people openly mocked the queen's absence. At one point, someone posted a *For Let* sign—the British equivalent of *For Rent*—on the gates of Buckingham Palace. It read "These commanding premises to be let or sold, in consequence of the late occupant's declining business." In other words: The queen was not doing her job.

Albert's death obviously left a void for Victoria not only in her personal life but also in her political life. Since becoming queen nearly a quarter century before, she had relied on advisers such as King Leopold, Lord Melbourne, and

Albert. But Leopold was far away in Belgium,
Melbourne had died in 1848, and now Albert had
died, too. She was alone.

In need of a shoulder on which to lean, Victoria turned to a servant named John Brown. He was from the Scottish Highlands, near Balmoral Castle. Brown became Victoria's favorite servant and companion. She liked him because, unlike other people, he was not intimidated by her. He was blunt and not afraid to speak his mind. Brown had constant access to the

BALMORAL CASTLE

queen, which did not sit well with much of the household.

Later, Victoria also found a great friend in Benjamin Disraeli, the prime minister in 1868, and then again from 1874 to 1880. Disraeli knew how to charm and flatter Victoria, and he also was an effective prime minister. He helped pass important legislation regarding child labor, public health, and sanitation.

"DIZZY" DISRAELI

PRIME MINISTER BENJAMIN DISRAELI WAS A FAVORITE OF QUEEN VICTORIA IN PART BECAUSE OF HIS SHARP SENSE OF HUMOR AND CLEVER CONVERSATION. HERE ARE A FEW OF "DIZZY'S" MEMORABLE SAYINGS.

TO AN AUTHOR HE DID NOT LIKE, WHEN PRESENTED ONE OF HIS BOOKS: "I SHALL WASTE NO TIME IN READING [IT]."

ON HOW TO TALK TO THE QUEEN: "EVERYONE LIKES FLATTERY, AND WHEN YOU COME TO ROYALTY, YOU SHOULD LAY IT ON WITH A TROWEL."

WHEN ASKED IF HE WOULD LIKE QUEEN VICTORIA TO VISIT HIM ON HIS DEATHBED IN 1881: "NO, IT IS BETTER NOT. SHE WOULD ONLY ASK ME TO TAKE A MESSAGE TO ALBERT."

Disraeli became a trusted adviser, and he worked hard to convince the queen to return to public life. It pleased Victoria very much when he introduced the Royal Titles Act of 1876, which bestowed on the queen the title empress of India. Victoria liked the title so much that she often signed her correspondence with it after that.

Victoria hired Indian servants and learned to love Indian culture, but she never actually set foot in India.

THE BRITISH IN INDIA

BY THE TIME QUEEN VICTORIA WAS NAMED EMPRESS OF INDIA, PEOPLE FROM GREAT BRITAIN HAD BEEN LIVING AND WORKING IN INDIA FOR NEARLY THREE HUNDRED YEARS.

IN 1600, THE EAST INDIA TRADING COMPANY WAS FOUNDED BY LONDON MERCHANTS WHO WERE TRADING IN THE REGION KNOWN AS THE EAST INDIES, BUT MAINLY THE COUNTRY OF INDIA. THE COMPANY SHIPPED LARGE QUANTITIES OF COTTON, SILK, SALT, AND TEA. IT HAD ITS OWN PRIVATE ARMY. THE EAST INDIA TRADING COMPANY USED ITS ARMY TO TAKE OVER POLITICAL RULE IN INDIA WHEN MAJOR GENERAL ROBERT CLIVE'S SMALL BRITISH ARMY DEFEATED A MUCH LARGER ARMY OF BENGAL TROOPS AND THEIR FRENCH ALLIES IN THE BATTLE OF PLASSEY.

IN 1857, INDIAN TROOPS REBELLED AGAINST THE
RULE OF THE EAST INDIA TRADING COMPANY.
AFTER THE REBELLION WAS DEFEATED, INDIA CAME
UNDER DIRECT RULE OF THE BRITISH GOVERNMENT.
INDIA FINALLY GAINED INDEPENDENCE FROM THE
UNITED KINGDOM IN 1947.

Chapter 8
Later Years

As Victoria's children grew and had children of their own, her offspring married into royal families throughout the European continent, including those in Germany, Spain, Norway, Russia, and more. Queen Victoria became known as the Grandmother of Europe.

Princess Victoria, Queen Victoria's first child, married German emperor Frederick III in 1858. They had a son, Wilhelm II. Ironically, it was Queen Victoria's grandson, Kaiser Wilhelm II, who later led Germany against Britain in World War I.

Bertie, Queen Victoria's first son, married Princess Alexandra of Denmark. Their daughter Maud became queen consort (wife of a reigning king) of Norway. Maud's son, Olav V, and grandson, Harald V, became kings of Norway.

PRINCESS
ALEXANDRA

MAUD

OLAV V

BERTIE

Of course, connections to Great Britain could be found all over the globe just by looking at the size of the British Empire. A country's empire includes all the places outside its own borders that are under its rule. During the Victorian era, Britain built the largest empire the world had ever seen. Its citizens traveled to faraway places to establish trading outposts on many of the major

THE BRITISH EMPIRE DURING THE VICTORIAN ERA

shipping routes around the world. They brought the English language, customs, and system of government with them. They established colonies that were under the rule of Great Britain and Queen Victoria.

Many of the world's empires grew through wars and military domination. The British Empire was not built for military purposes, however.

It grew mainly through trade and manufacturing. The British Empire was able to take raw goods from its colonies and produce manufactured goods in Great Britain, creating great wealth. Great Britain's navy was important because it protected merchant ships along the trading routes, and its famous red-coated army helped keep the peace in places far from England.

By the time Queen Victoria celebrated her Golden Jubilee—her fiftieth anniversary as queen—in 1887, Great Britain had become known as the Workshop of the World. Britain produced more manufactured goods than any other place in the world.

Victoria's Golden Jubilee celebration was an exciting two-day event. The king of Denmark and the king of Greece were among fifty European kings, queens, and royals who attended the royal banquet at Buckingham Palace.

The next day, Victoria rode in a procession through the streets of London, with crowds cheering her all along the way. That night, she enjoyed a huge fireworks display from her garden at the palace.

Abdul Karim of India was neither a diplomat nor a prince, but he arrived as a servant to a delegation of Indian princes at the queen's Golden Jubilee celebration. Abdul Karim stayed in England, and the queen hired him as a servant. He soon

ABDUL KARIM

became her favorite servant, much as John Brown had before him. Victoria called him "the Munshi," which means teacher in Hindustani, and enjoyed her Indian servant's colorful costumes and white turbans. She began taking lessons in Hindustani from the Munshi. But as with John Brown, who had died in 1883, the Munshi's status didn't sit well with the rest of the household. They did not trust him and were afraid he was trying to take advantage of Victoria. The queen didn't pay any attention to the rest of her staff, however, and she remained very loyal to her Munshi.

Nine years later, in 1896, Victoria became the longest-reigning monarch in Britain's history at the time, surpassing her grandfather, George III.

The very next year, she celebrated sixty years on the throne. Victoria's Diamond Jubilee lasted two weeks! More than thirteen hundred people from around the world sent telegrams of congratulations.

The queen was seventy-eight years old by then, however, and her health had begun to suffer.

Over the next few years, Victoria's public appearances became increasingly rare. In May 1899, she performed one of her last public duties, dedicating the cornerstone for what would become the Victoria and Albert Museum in London.

By 1900, she was having trouble walking, her eyesight became very poor, and she suffered several strokes.

Queen Victoria died at age eighty-one on January 22, 1901. Upon her death, her eldest son, Bertie, became King Edward VII.

Before Victoria passed, she arranged the details for her own funeral. After thirty-nine years of wearing only black, she requested that she be buried in white because the time for mourning was over. She would soon be reunited with her beloved Albert.

Chapter 9
Legacy

At 63 years and 216 days, Queen Victoria had one of the longest reigns of any monarch in Britain's history. She had nine children, and outlived three of them: Alice died at thirty-five in 1878; Leopold died at thirty in 1884;

and Alfred died at fifty-five in 1900. She had forty grandchildren and thirty-seven great-grandchildren at the time of her death! Ten different prime ministers served the United Kingdom during her reign.

THE SUN NEVER SETS ON THE BRITISH EMPIRE

QUEEN VICTORIA REIGNED OVER NOT ONLY THE PEOPLE IN THE UNITED KINGDOM BUT ALSO ALL THE PEOPLE IN THE BRITISH EMPIRE—TERRITORIES AROUND THE WORLD THAT WERE UNDER BRITISH POLITICAL CONTROL.

DURING VICTORIA'S TIME AS QUEEN, THE BRITISH EMPIRE EXPANDED GREATLY. DURING HER REIGN, IT GREW TO ENCOMPASS ONE-QUARTER OF THE EARTH'S LANDMASS, INCLUDING A POPULATION OF NEARLY FOUR HUNDRED MILLION PEOPLE IN EUROPE, AFRICA, ASIA, AND THE AMERICAS. THE BRITISH EMPIRE ALSO INCLUDED CANADA, WHICH DID NOT GAIN INDEPENDENCE UNTIL 1867, AND AUSTRALIA, PART OF WHICH WAS FIRST CLAIMED FOR THE BRITISH BY EXPLORER JAMES COOK IN 1770.

IN 1829, A SCOTTISH JOURNALIST POPULARIZED THE SAYING "THE SUN NEVER SETS ON THE BRITISH EMPIRE," MEANING THAT THE EMPIRE WAS SO VAST THAT IT WAS ALWAYS DAYLIGHT ON BRITISH PEOPLE SOMEWHERE.

Victoria's legacy, though, is much more than one of endurance. The Victorian era was a largely peaceful and prosperous one for Great Britain. On Victoria's watch, many important changes took place in manufacturing, engineering, science, and medicine.

Britain's Joseph Lister introduced antiseptic surgery in the 1860s. He used carbolic acid to help sterilize instruments, clean wounds, and reduce infections.

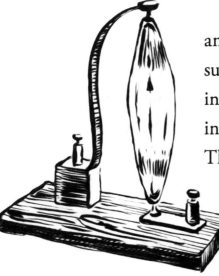

British physicist and chemist Joseph Swan successfully tested an incandescent lightbulb in 1878, one year before Thomas Edison revealed his own lightbulb in the United States.

The adhesive postage stamp came into being during the Victorian era. Naturally, the first stamp, in 1840, bore an image of the queen.

In 1858, Victoria sent the first official telegram from one continent to another when she wired United States president James Buchanan. Twenty years later, Victoria became the first British monarch to use the telephone. She tried the telephone at Osborne House with help from its inventor, Scotland's Alexander Graham Bell.

Queen Victoria also was the first monarch to be photographed. Ironically, though, photography was one area in which advancements didn't come fast enough during Victoria's time. Although the world's first photograph was taken in 1826, for many decades cameras were big and bulky, and shutter speeds were painfully slow. No one could be expected to hold a smile for the many minutes it took to capture a still portrait.

Victoria and Albert did purchase photographic portraits in the 1840s and 1850s. But most of the surviving photos of Victoria show her in mourning attire after Albert's death, many from her years as an aging queen. They create a lasting impression of a solemn person: a sad woman and a strict ruler.

Drawings and paintings of the queen as a young woman, however, as well as her journal and letters, reveal a spirited and energetic monarch eager to lead her people. It is *that* Victoria who was the foundation for one of the most important and influential eras in world history.

QUEEN ELIZABETH II

THE UNITED KINGDOM'S MOST RECENT QUEEN
WAS ELIZABETH II. ELIZABETH II WAS BORN IN
1926 AND WAS ONLY TWENTY-FIVE YEARS OLD
WHEN SHE BECAME THE QUEEN. SHE WAS THE

ELDEST DAUGHTER OF KING GEORGE VI AND QUEEN ELIZABETH. HER GRANDFATHER WAS KING GEORGE V, WHO WAS THE SON OF BERTIE, QUEEN VICTORIA'S ELDEST SON. THAT MAKES QUEEN ELIZABETH II A GREAT-GREAT-GRANDDAUGHTER OF QUEEN VICTORIA.

SHE ASCENDED TO THE THRONE IN 1952 AND REIGNED FOR SEVENTY YEARS—LONGER THAN ANYONE ELSE IN BRITISH HISTORY.

TIMELINE OF
QUEEN VICTORIA'S LIFE

1819 — Born Alexandrina Victoria on May 24 at Kensington Palace in London, England

1837 — On June 20, becomes queen after the death of her uncle, William IV

1838 — Is officially crowned the queen at ceremonies at Westminster Abbey

1839 — Feuds with incoming prime minister Sir Robert Peel in the Bedchamber Crisis

1840 — Marries Prince Albert on February 10
Princess Victoria, who is called Vicky, is born November 21

1841 — Gives birth to her first son, Albert Edward (also known as Bertie), on November 9

1851 — The Great Exhibition is held in London

1857 — Princess Beatrice, the last of Queen Victoria and Prince Albert's nine children (five girls and four boys), is born on April 14

1861 — Prince Albert dies on December 14 at age forty-two

1866 — After nearly five years, Queen Victoria makes her first public appearance since the death of Prince Albert when she presides over the opening of Parliament

1876 — With the help of Prime Minister Disraeli, Queen Victoria ends her long period of withdrawal from public life

1877 — Adds the title empress of India

1887 — Celebrates fifty years (Golden Jubilee) as queen

1897 — Celebrates sixty years (Diamond Jubilee) as queen

1901 — Dies on January 22 at age eighty-one

TIMELINE OF THE WORLD

Britain and the United States wage the War of 1812 — **1812**

US president James Monroe outlines the Monroe Doctrine, calling for an end to European interference in the Western Hemisphere — **1823**

Mexico becomes a republic — **1824**

The California gold rush begins — **1849**

The Crimean War begins when Turkey declares war on Russia; Britain and France join the conflict in 1854 — **1853**

The Civil War in the United States begins — **1861**

General Robert E. Lee surrenders his Confederate forces at Appomattox, effectively ending the US Civil War; US president Abraham Lincoln is assassinated — **1865**

Alfred Nobel invents dynamite — **1866**

Thomas Edison invents the first commercially practical incandescent light — **1879**

US president James Garfield is assassinated — **1881**

New Zealand becomes the first modern nation to give women the right to vote — **1893**

German physicist Wilhelm Röntgen discovers X-rays — **1895**

In the United States, the Supreme Court's *Plessy v. Ferguson* decision establishes the segregation doctrine of "separate but equal" — **1896**

The British fight the Boer War in South Africa against descendants of Dutch settlers — **1899**

BIBLIOGRAPHY

*Chiflet, Jean-Loup and Beaulet, Alain. **Victoria and Her Times**. New York: Henry Holt and Company, 1996.

*Green, Robert. **Queen Victoria**. New York: Franklin Watts, 1998.

*Guy, John. **Queen Victoria**. United Kingdom: Ticktock Publishing Ltd., 1998.

Hibbert, Christopher. **Queen Victoria: A Personal History**. New York: Basic Books, 2000.

Hubbard, Kate. **Serving Victoria: Life in the Royal Household**. London: Chatto & Windus, 2012.

Jaffé, Deborah. **Victoria: A Celebration**. London: Carlton Books Limited, 2000.

*Shearman, Deirdre. **Queen Victoria (World Leaders Past & Present)**. New Haven, CT: Chelsea House Publishers, 1986.

Strachey, Lytton. **Queen Victoria (An Eminent Illustrated Biography)**. New York: Black Dog & Leventhal Publishers, Inc., 1998.

*Whitelaw, Nancy. **Queen Victoria and the British Empire**. Greensboro, NC: Morgan Reynolds Publishing, Inc., 2005.

*Books for young readers

YOUR HEADQUARTERS FOR HISTORY

Activities, Mad Libs, and sidesplitting jokes!
Discover the Who HQ books beyond the biographies

Who? What? Where?

Learn more at whohq.com!